WORDS FOR JOY BUT OF SORROW
THE YEAR 1957

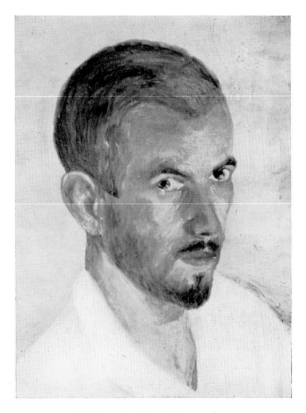

Self-portrait of the author

Words for Joy but of Sorrow
The Year 1957

ANDERSON NETTLESHIP

THE SHAKESPEARE HEAD PRESS
ETON, WINDSOR

1958

Printed by
The Ditchling Press Limited
Ditchling, Hassocks, Sussex

TO LOIS

Whose love and memory built
a world of golden light.

CONTENTS

PART I

PART II

INTRODUCTORY NOTES

THE HUBRIS of our existence lies in the myth of man's invincibility. Our ultimate wrong is the disregard of man, as person and kin.

Mass man and modern barbarians are readily swayed by the false custodians of, their neglected rights. The malevolent swipe of mortal man leaves no avenue for escape of man.

Spiritual affinities and past traditions of great beauty are discarded in favour of a cardboard existence. The meaningless thirties give way to the lost forties and the fifties pay for an ill-gotten debt.

Today's poetry is vigilant of the almost forgotten spoken and chanted music of the ancients, but often, in an ambiguous and hostile environment, misses the flavour of nature's more meaningful rhythms, the vital poetry which swept earlier man with visions of generative beliefs so profound that to be contra nature was not a part of him. It may have been necessary for man to placate his gods and in another time romanticize his position but it has never before been his role to destroy his own spirit. Today's being stands thus shorn, seemingly without fundamental need.

The ways of nature are here and cannot be denied. Man's ways will again become therein a part or man will not be.

ANDERSON NETTLESHIP

Little Rock, Arkansas, U.S.A.

March 15, 1957

PART I

SALAMANDER

Winter's wet sod of south
  warm,
To be dug through drizzle and grey.
In black sod where turned
  a salamander coiled,
With lazy tact filled his space,
  quiet,
Light fog lifted past.
I dug earth
A clod broke, there he lay
Slick, dark, brown body chameleon
  slick, black streaked
  white beneath
  closed lids but
When the clod broke eyes opened,
  he uncoiled, coiled, moved beneath a clod.
Odd in this of places and times
Of a world, a whole universe
In this sod, this space, chimeral flesh.

STONEHENGE

Faint today the shadows cast by Quagga,
  Ancient Ring broken.
Unheeded builders of megalith
  The People of Stonehenge scattered.
Too brief their time and the harvest time
  brings shallow markings.
Henge and the last Romans
They dwelt outward,
A sunlit plain.

OCTOBER—HALLOWE'EN

The flying masks
  Children laugh
    We caught a brief list of curved bowl of
      immortality,
This hurt and I did cry.

A LITANY TO MOHENJO-DARO

> This writing is to portray something of a
> forgotten empire of antiquity. It is of a
> liturgical nature: to what? Neither
> religion nor science contains adequate
> explanation of the origin, growth and
> death of civilizations. Can any religion
> explain this occurrence? Can bio-
> archaeology, with its concepts of 1,500
> year cycles, give cause why people can
> group together to form such rich, start-
> lingly beautiful moites, only to be utterly
> destroyed and with them the key to their
> existence? Hence this writing.

The Indus flows, flowed.
The lion and lioness prowl,
Karachi the city. The priests of
Mohenjo-Daro no longer lithy walk platforméd citadels,
Harappa destroyed.

The Greek and Imperator knew this fragile flower, pollen pod of
Tiber Apollos and
Belvedere. Archaic Greek and else that
  followed flowed from this kingdom,
  the Indus.

14

A Litany to Mohenjo-Daro

Marked alone, unique, clear and crisp culture
    the way to society, Harappan Civilization.

Now the dust, terrible caking dust over and
    overlying all, walls, palaces, vineyards, fields,
    villages, city, graves and wooden
    coffins.
Precise grid work, their cities, no nomad shacks.
Streets and homes of well-fired brick, the public granary and
    bath, the cloistered couch and pillared
    hall.
People. The joy of sunlight and rains,
Rulers not, only quiet priests.
Workmen and the inevitable pottery, a pot
    to put something in.
Those of clay, round, well-turned, amphoric,
Designs red and black on clay, beautiful
    then in freshness.
Beautiful now when all
    the clay has bone-lost its colour.
Red and black, sprightly and clearly struck in clay.
A place now for water, milk, grain.
And the graven images of bisque, head-dresses, platen eyes
    stuck on the face, child's play.
Not the rest. Well-rounded shoulders,
    great breasts and well-rounded omphalos.
Fertility goddesses, that our wives may be fertile,
    our children many. We shall clothe these in
    shining necklace, breastplate, ringing head-dress.
For God. The Apollo Tiber.
These shall be fired, these our record.
Delicate now and peaceful for we are a people.
Then we shall do the torse. In its
    umber limbs a tongue of flame not yet dead, not dead today.

Harappa the triangle finished. Valley of the Indus,
Valley of the Tigris-Euphrates and of the Nile.

A Litany to Mohenjo-Daro

Nameless, forgotten.
High culture, high priests, high intellect.
The circle, the square, the angle, the right angle and
    smolten bronze.
In their valley plush green, the ocean edge and beyond
    valley foothills of snow-capped Himalayas.
The Ravi tributaries.
Empire, Empire gone.
Now the rains, heavy the steaming jungles,
    monkeys cry, constrictor kills. The tiger,
    copper and bronze. Precious metals. Gold and jewellery.
The wheel.
And wonderful accurate measures.
From here to the corner and back, from this unto that by
    exact weight.

Millenium Millenium Millenium
The agony of birth.

We are no longer wanderers. We have arrived.
Now our love-beds lie behind secure walls,
    our women stand in their rooms flesh
    proud.
Our life now no flood can destroy, the inundations
    cleanse the city.
No more the stench of the wanderer's
    tent.

Script and sculpture, seal engravings.
Life and Traditions. Man as first true urban man.

Love.

No defence.

Annihilate.

Our writing, pictographic, a stiff hieroglyph;
  directions and things we should have done.
Supplications to the lost gods. Oh, Monsoon God!
Gentle and destroyed.
We walked the distance but it did no good. These
  our priests, our gods. Piety and obligates.

Puce now the land and our homes.
Pudendum and our love. Dead the ecstasy. Courtyard not in
  sweet shadow but blank dirt and sorrow.
No longer men with sweat from
  fields and maidens wait in milk-white woven cloth.
    The terrace, warped empty.
The quick end. No more the pleasant moon nor
  sun. No more child's cry or cattle lowing.

The grave pitch calls.
Pre-Siva strength overworn.
Disease. War. Famine, Vandal, Iconoclast. The springs of race
  run down,
  or unlikely God's call.
The square tomb filth-ridden, a twilight.
Obscurity.
Forget.

DESTINY—THE WASTE PLACE

I.

Unleash the dogs singing swinging over the dry hills,
  Saluqis racing the new moon.
Afgod in the burning bush.
Flint-flakes under the nim-tree
Elam and Sumer.

Leaves of the sacred pipal tree are blown by the
    faint breeze,
Auroch urus-bull
Mother goddess alabaster.
Limestone demi-god, man-bull.
    That torn sherd
    Desert of the Sind
    Place of the Dead.

    Linga yonis
    Hot butter and cool water
    Blood and oil.

There's no more time,
There is no more time and the yew tree cries
    for war's track, flagrante bello, leaves nor man.
Man brute when rain drops and hollow helmets rust,
in the yellow-green mud streaks red blood
    And the sovereign cries! parlously!
Syrinx of raven's caw turned into Pan's pipe
    Not to escape pain of love
But its loss.

Moving softly she stood
Soft pink maiden's hair high.

II.

The cold moles dig deep in artica,
Anapopei hot sand
Where men lie flat to escape the screech fragments,
    shrapnel.
Chosen war and glass fibre vests do not protect
    membrum virile.
Paraplegics, the breast paraorgasm does not
    suffice for man-woman.

We went down the docks. In the East River on
   Sunday morning were grapefruits floats, bald
   yellow heads beneath the water and jelly fish
   domes grey filled. Kismet laughed and
   said what a way to end up or down?

People in the country-side to town. They
did not return. Machines came.
Strangers now live in the country.
America table vast, city accretions,
   nexus bound by twin hasps of iron.
Almagordo our Armageddon!

   Images flicker in the lined light.
   The puppets jerk
   expose their bottoms
   Breasts bulge
   Lights wear thin
   flicker
   White on the couch yields
   against the green mohair.
   She's really too tired.

   'There is no sense in it I tell you,
   I told you last night it was all over
     And now you want to go on."

III.

Ocarina sweet clay moulding dulcet notes
Ocarina honey song in the dust of hot southern sun.
Jujube! jujube! jujube!

Taffy pulling butter-scotch in northern delights
Cold snow winds in the hill folds
Old bitterness, sour.

19

Odour of moon-moth wings against the moon's
    trumpet vine,
Ambrosia and spices of redolent
    perfumed night.

How often I have lain with silvery music Hyblaean
Fair and comely thy shape
Winsome and loving thy charm,
Gentle thy hand and tempered welcome.

IV.

Desert waste. No longer red-bird's song but
    sound of mushroom sorcerer. Faint then
    across the shattered desert rising scale in wild polyphonic
    reverberations. No clear modulation or key but
    broken catacoustic on ejected void.
                        Bomb-carol-fission.

Summer storms, sheet lightning, monsters
    gelatinoids against sky dark cast.
    The purple strangle.
    No rain.
    The waste land extends, exterminates.

The cords, the golden cords are broken!
It must have been a harp;
The cream white plaster ran into
holes and filled its gracious shape. Then
cords aurum rang and wild agony of this loss
was too much for the malmute who ran across
the site, shot dead.

V.

They lay abed, askew. His finger plucked a
    turgid string.

Soon they played, the rhythm sange a clysmic tune,
Clear fluid, juices of earth.
The sky was split with silver lance
Beautiful sheath unfolds, white
    metal drops
  the parts together and holds.
The woman shudders, is sickly, shuns
  the light.
The smooth ball settles, slides earthward
    Sudden, shrieking, shrill scream
    The rumpled shroud, winding sheet, cerecloth.

VI.

Man and son sit beside quiet bassano
Still water holds tree, and sky above,
  first sense of autumn.
A lone pigeon flutters,
A lone leaf loose turns from limb to ground,
Child smiles and views all, including man.
Leaf plucked, soft grey feather thrust mid shaft and
  graceful boat takes to ocean, mirror bassano,
The air carries boat, leaf, manson.

Oh sweet pod broken!

THE GOLDEN PLUM TREE

Dust and the oil well flat land come to the tangled
  briar's edge,
Here the green rivers flow,
Beyond the hills begin
  and trees' foliage.
On valley sides the dogwoods bloom.

The Golden Plum Tree

Spring's robin cries and moisture seeps the ground.
Hickory smoke of autumn's past is smell memory
    and
There are small mounds of white washed stones
    clean in creek-beds.

The hedgerow blooms
Cocks crow, close then faint.
Tumult dies, music carries over trees,
Woman goes achild-bed with clenched teeth and screams,
    Bloody gout.
The new-born peeks out
The world awearying.

Fields grow rye celadon
    Small virgin beards on milky seeds,
    Rows turn at corner field.

In run of our low bushes, in canopy of sky,
    The Plum.
Fresh leaves spear heads shaking chill in
    spring wind.
White mist of blossoms delicate haze,
    Fertile bee pressing home attacks beyond court or count
Flagrant noviate violent.

Crystal morn,
The male child born
Male child and sweet woman hurt.

Cares torn
Day's drone,
The downy lip
Open door. Afternoon fey.

    Across the field, bush rows end in the Golden Plum.
By Obi into circle Ob.

The Golden Plum Tree

Beaten nest the unshared haven
   quiet sanctuary, no cry of torture heard.
The child's eye in union with self. The nest of self.

The warm olive plums growing
   meat. Temptation to bite, knowing simmon
   drawing juice tight on teeth and gums.

Time slowage.

Palamino brown horse, sweat of thigh, black eyes and mane
   flying dirt clods from bare hooves.
Rain, smatter of dust in the nostrils from summer's dusty road,
Melodious sob of turtle-dove.
Gracious bend of full limbs
Bark of brown satin, birds-eye flecked,
Trunk felt in security.
Tears of misery clod wetting the nourishment of plum.
Twist and blur of hurt past hurt.
Gore gone.

The skin tart,
Rich red pulp filling sugarplum skin to bursting
Golden ones firm, high treasure to the hand,
Seeds pointed and curved with
   labial edges.

In earth goblets hollow mashed fruit fallen
Plum with skin split by stinger thrust,
Milden sour smell. Fall and the plum skin full.
Plum   Pulp   Seed.

The black limbs bare against winter sky
   and white.
Winter's limbs bare black.

SUN-FLIGHT

Summer's long melody
   Bee flight, sun-dust pollen wings
Drunken libation impelled against sweet sprung
   rut of thy Queen.
Sun-speared in echoed mad mounting flight
   Slave to Sun's most primal urge.
Last of thy race in drunken carousel quaffed,
   Seal of death.

Queen floating from shade into noontide sunlight,
   With all pell-mell in mad-bee flight after,
Rising dark spiral shattered by lamed and foiled going down.

Piercing strain of coquette's gesture lusting in
   blue sky,
Queen now in frenzied frantic flight circles last heights and
   here the prince finds her,
Sobbing hymn.

Sudden lunge and billion cells,
   Stinger pull in final agony,
Falls the hollow hulk.

Lazy queen glides
Sun into shadow, laden cells await, engulf,
   Soft abdomen, slow abandon.

CREATIVE MAN

In Races' taut hour, at war or peace Death's
   windrows pile high,
With bodies stacked.

Creative Man

Chance from these spared a brief throb,
   Imbedded in no culture, or clime,
In whose threads creation converges.
Unblurred, unhurried souls, splendidly composed.
Their most precious gift to ascertain unseen shattered places and
   to rebel.
Widely, wildly a throbbing spectrum, their fruits
   delight us.
Their work unpaid and most oft unsought.
Not for pride, nor pence, nor love, nor praise
But for the doing they live.
Their humble arts of Earth and Ages
   Rise from dirt to move unlettered plowman and
      sway the great.
Eroding rustless ties they free the soul.

Not apostles with godhead or motive but
   breakers of Time's continuum,
   Spiller and spoiler of Time's content,
     And from its shreds
Prepare wonders wondrously.
Sorrowful I am that born when life is cold formula
And milk and juice there is no more. Not even
   the spring green or the cold mist in springs cold
   water.
Not water clear the streams on sacred virgin
   banks or the dallying.
All life, all juices, all Donne's gone.

Now we repair to hollow empty rooms,
   couched in torn rags suck the pabulum of
   dogs not men.
The rich pear, the open melon with splendid slick
   seeds. The sweet rhyme of maiden's lips and
   laughing hips.
The rain.
The earth moisture rises unnoticed. We shall get our feet
   wet, oh damn. Not even a hearty word left us!

Born at time when life is two plus two,
Await now the press of years,
When frenzied naked men fall on own spears,
These spaces when all static life is formalized,
Cenogenesis fails and
Each coin must two sides.
Only a silversmith with new gold and tools to save the dust.

Undone until the magic cycle encycles cycles and
    jerks therefrom the gifted one who
Standing stark strikes lustre anew from standstill clay.

A POEM FOR JOY AND OF SORROW

Spindrift sky of high mid-west
Sheer argent streamers of feather crystals blown
    Flowing free, high in hoarfrost sky,
    In the still air.

It is cold,
The sleek crows' call on town's edge.
Shadow sides of pine hills in the spring
Rising air chill against new green branches.

The warmth of spring on earth,
Leisure buds open, white. Star white of
    Bethlehem, iris purple and yellow,
    Buttercups and maiden's pinks,
    Sheeps-sorrel spice to tongue.

Against horizons in the south an albic curved stroke,
Quick thrown tight but fragile skein,
At first more sensed than seen.
Then gone.

A Poem for Joy and of Sorrow

Next day clear, at first faint whitening commas against blue
  Now chalk tracks knotted direct overhead, small silver lancet,
    high thrown
With such great skill and after it
Twin candent trailers putting out to hold
  Silver spearhead.
Solomon's plume in the dry land
And far away noise, a whine,
The spun wail call of man's last call to man.

Little moths carrying.

Seared flesh of man well cooked by the
  naphthalene burst of molten fire,
The deadly blast killer
or heat
or fire
or radiation,
or, most subtle the poison carried in
air into man's lungs into his intimate
blood.
To destroy his blood.

Then daily now the white hooked streaks, very
  precise, mind you.
As though they came from
draftsman's board,
    They did.

No let-up, streaks came every day, twice or
  thrice a day, shattering our visual peace.
The drawn ivory lines float with such care toward
  earth's flange,
Ragged scars across once peaceful sky to soon blend
  with sky.
We are told, it's necessary to give practice
  so they drop the bomb with great accuracy.
No longer worry or look into sky, the sound is far away.

A Poem for Joy and of Sorrow

Little silvery moths climb the sky, bent crosses leave their
    trails, are gone.
We were not certain where they came, argai why worry,
Always there
Close Summer's heat, they were there,
Fall's coloured leaves, they were there.
Sad creamed mid-winter china-berries on leafless boughs,
    They came overhead, an unravelled thread across
    the winter sky.
Etiolate cross thrown free.

Later!

The day came, the clouds came.
Great billows against the ground,
    by sunset sky streaks blood red,
Splashed in pink streamers against earth's far western
    edge.
Etched against early winter's dark clouds.
    White streaks slash the top of this
    from crater of sunset into the shallows of moon rise,
    White streaks slash.
No telling God made and which by
    man.

Where have you been?
    I've been to the hole to see, guess, yes, Mike
And what did you there?
    I frightened the little mouse (?) in the
hole's bottom.

THE HEART'S SCARAB

Great green scarab climbs into the heart's chambers
    and
Winter rains cold lash across
Wet sodden earth and lance
    my heart,
And leave empty the hearthstone
    of my existence.

PARADE

Spring, cold grey skies and colourful parade
Baseball god,
The parade and young girls clean bare legs unscarred
Aching so to be hurt and hence marked
    by Pan or Faustian spring,
Satyr with cloved hoof.

WHITE MARBLES IN THE PINK BEGONIA
BLOSSOM HEADS

OR

EASTER AT THE SEA-SIDE RESORT,
ATLANTIC CITY

We were playing at tea
We were playing at tea at the sea
Blood of St Dennis in the hall
And early season's cold made us under coat,
Though our heads were onion-burned and hurt.
Like pink begonias. Though pink begonias for Easter call
But Cathy said they're really not you know they're
    hydrangeas,
Hydrangeas strangers with white marbles in their heads.
Pink ladies on a spool are unwound thread.
With the cameras clicking, clicking at the dummies
    posed on the boardwalk.

In trying to reach across the chambered nautilus crushed
    in its hollow shell,
Close in, closing, no longer communicate, or a
    communicant with Easter sunday unholy on
the seaside resort and ships funnel down, dirty
      smoke smudge on the sea's edge.

Resentful of you beside me, and the evening tide now
    clean and cold and green?
There is no more often seen or said than
    alabaster water breaking across the dark night,
      coming here, spring's year.
With spring's year in spray with fog banks
    have often seen this tide,
        Atlantic.
Walking in sand shoe high then wet packed hard.

Lonely and sea gulls or lonely and the night with
   white breakers,
Far out, then coming quickly in leaving
   their splashed filigree shore's edge.
Here alone and silent music lonely.
Hence when you came I found this strange
And was resentful at intrusion.

   In holy rolling conclave the waves keep
dark passage.

SPRING PURPLE AFTER THE BOMB

Pitiful now with red bud's bloom in spring
   no poet remains to say,
Spring melody! Spray of purple blossoms on black branches
      fragile,
Flush of fingered purple o'er May apples and in still
   void woodland
These filamentous purples will fade,
These blossoms will wither and quickly too, for already
   the poison dust has filled earth's good air
   with
Empty cities
Stench of flesh
The shadow men.
   (I gave up this spirit illy and with reluctance.)

Cry not in pessimism,
But cry! Cry!

For all the living flower is gone.

The college boys did die
Did die the college girls

At first not.
But now.

To death, to indifferent death then and the
   Eternal cycle.
Bomb blast or heat or rapid radiation or
   slow,
Take the poison gently, breathe it quietly, it hurts not,
Good blood's domain invade, destroy,
Now we have water in our veins.

The last cenotaph, empty tomb, and last processionals
of frantic Battuti have
   walked into their graves.
The last worm soaks their watered flesh.

I SHALL HAVE YOU IN ALL WILD OZARK
ENCAMPMENTS

In moist depths, in the chill water springs naked
Against the warm bark on south side of trees,
   In earliest spring facing west,
On high Ozark escarpments.
   I shall love you.
In the west yellow haze and blazing sun molt
Desert to the west, but rich secure
   green at back.

In cabins and courtyards in resorts
Yellow bulb glowing alone across the dark courtyard,
Love candle in resort dark.

Or knowing swift killing grace of wines fair
To go abed with thee sweet Sue.

On hearing bird's restless twitter in the false light to stand
With feet in wet dew grass,
   To love the lost and trembling flesh.

POMEGRANATE TREE. OUR LOVE IN A GARDEN

In the plein-air
Pomegranates hang from spiked limbs in late summer
   Mustard, cloves and sharp spikenard,
   The season's ballet sings through the plein-air
 Through open window the woman's breasts with milk swell,
   lean forward in silken clasp on window ledge.
Peregrine voices proliferate, pit-a-pat across garden's
   spaces,
Sounds etched by pleasant acid flesh of pomegranate rind.

Globed fruit holding in pink acropolis
   Dreams of Taj-Mahal.

Pome flower sound
Woman full of angels and deceit,
Eve of this abode,
Of all Eternity.

Morning horn blown on the dry woods,
Fountains wash silver coins new.
Her flesh clothes closely soul and
   marvellous parts ring softly, soft woman
   flesh, full, prenatal.

Feeling running rich,
Empty, then, and again,
Known woman.
Love. Drink and food through more and more.
More than you can have but want and live,
Possess now.
That which ends.
Slowly and by magic again,
Happy hymn.

Into black sensoria, into reality, into
    reality beyond.

Content, without tragedy
She loves.

The afternoon's focus.

SCHIST OF SADNESS

I sit alone beside the rain and know this
    most heart-breaking,
These raindrops fall and
    I hear
On slick roof, green leaves, tree trunk, grass, stones,
    in lum of dirt soft
    in splash on slate rock
    and on pavement drill,
The raindrops fall.
And I shall die and the raindrops shall
    fall on all these sounds,
Soft and hard.
Raindrops fall,
To hear them, hunger of my dust, is
    beyond bearing.

GOLDEN BUD

Oh, the Golden Bud,
Man's direst need, Love.

MUSCA VOLTANTES, PINK SLOWLIES
A POEM FOR ONE MIMI

Today they look like a rabbit so, squatted and
    with ears like hands held over head.
Yesterday they were little broken worms floating
    free,
Tomorrow they shall be.
The next days with eyes closed they float and
    yank from here to there.
    They're pink slowlies.

THE BOY'S MOON

The evening's trust of early fall.
Cool shadows with warm sun drawn, now
    crickets call
Across the road there's quarter acre of
    full butter beans, dry and
    picking soon to fill a barrel.
Tall poplar beyond the patch, its leaves flicker.

The evening quiet with peopled porches and
    front yards.
Aslant through the dark,
A child's plaint
Soft spoken voices mix and still the cricket's call.
Loosely on porch edge feet swinging.

The moon.

Then road's dust cool powder squeezed by boy toes
Big and pointing toe.
Road runs down hill into
A hill, East mountain.
Over, beyond East full moon, larger
    than before,
Silver.
Misted moon edges,
Gliding up the moon-silver.

Turn to moon,
For the first time boy is past the immediate
and knows feeling lost outside.

Moon and people at peace.
The sense of no longer being within being
but extending self beyond, near moon,
    spaces away.

No longer the boy. The moon.
Instead he looks unseeing ahead,
Turns, enters the yard, the house.
Past ever looking back again.

AGONY OF APART

This piece no pæan to loneliness
    I have known.
But agony of being from one I love.

The years apart, agony
The months between, agony
The weeks and days cry lonely agony,
The last hours horrors of despair,
Comes minutes of agony.

Slow drops cruelly drawn,
And lastly seconds of agony, of apart.

The shock of unbelief at your Being
Slowly wears off.
Things become ordinary again, the
Joints fit smoothly
The screaming edge lights disappear
from objects.
Things become commonplace
when agony is gone.

MR BRAHMS AND SUMMER LOVE

In sweat of field dust shaken from clothes
Walk through high grain, summer's heat.
And wash-pan of water to clean
the skin.
Ache of tired physical pain,
All senses awake, draw fine
The work done and mid-afternoon
the hot run.

Across sunlit field great trees blow
Tall, heavy-topped trees rich heads bend together smoothed
in south wind blowing north.
Lying in dark parlour on rug the quintet (f) plays,
Fine notes gathered in perfect
units of a single string.
They play music from the pen of
Mr Brahms.

Along the bush fences apricot blooms
Tender purple.
The day, condensed sun on fields and
blowing trees,
Music plays.

Not anguished love cries Schubert
Nor grandiose Beethoven.
Flameless tunes of white arcades
    marvellous,
Of swans stately arched, unruffled on
    quiet water
Are tunes carried across the field
    into blowing trees.
They call neither sad nor gay but
    music of certain love.
They tell of young man's first white
    arcaded love,
And forever music, immortal!

The night before, the day before and summers
    hence
This music ceased not, to marvel
    from it a whole fabric became,
Became a part of life, a part of
    music.
Heights of joy held in such
    vibrant lights
And sorrow flowed pregnant with sounds.
Music in June, July and August
    And entering September Fall.
It flew over all time into the room of
    love with first return to love.
Pæan funeral music, not a dirge,
In perfect spaces no
    sorrow,
Immaculate music!
Ah whirlwind of throbbing notes
Carry heights across unclouded
    field
With wind in tree heads
And the gladsome melody,
    Resonant!

SUNDAY STREETS

Once in Toronto, Canada, on a Sunday
Spring morning. Downtown a massed
phalanx of women dressed in dark death-
coloured clothes suddenly formed in the
street and marched in strict, close order,
carrying down the street frenetic religion
before them. Like the bugle-call of a
fatal flame, it shone in their eyes.

A strange godhead that would spill the horrors of
    night into Sunday morning streets.
Blows the wind in less penitent years
    but these destroy shed light,
And robe of light goes dead.
The shining clay becomes wormwood and as gall,
Canticle divine a crow's callous call.

Down Sunday's empty streets the
    black crows massed march,
Right, left
Right, left
White flesh through cotton stocks
Black graceless dress, coal-scuttle brims of
    scooped hats over pale faces
March insipid flesh,
March wan flesh to the chains of hell,
March to pale destiny.

On Sunday's empty streets the
    buildings grey
The litter swirls, debris of week's waste in
    empty spaces where the morning light falls
    between buildings and
On streets,
One hears loudly traffic light change,

39

Linking sense to sound and sight,
Red—CLICK
Yellow—CLICK
Green—CLICK
CLICK, CLICK, CLICK.

In empty streets the sound.

MID-WEEK IN THE SMALL HILLS

It is mid-week in the small green hills
The sense of Sunday gone, the
    bathéd sun
  The smell of milk in the
    countryside
  And the hill
    The clean chapel spires glow.
    Brightness of morning and
    in the shadows
A great black dog head guards
    the stone church portals.

A PIECE

There was quarrel and dirt at home
  but here it was better,
The girl in pink pyjamas walks beside
  the highway
Facing westward in the sun
The cars run toward her and past,
Long past the hurt, my darling.

LEAD

Rock-riddled shell and melted lead in
   the rock's parts,
Screech of fife across the green,
   the call
Of locusts in the trees.
Drum roll, fife pitch
Heart beat of the Revolution, he cried,

I go mourning in my heart
   all the day long.

THE RAINBOW

No dry tears
   Now
For tears, torn the flesh
The soul

No dry tears now
For tears.

One limb only with spectrum proud
   Shadow iridescent
      purple into orange-red,
      grey about.
In crib of its curve a lightning thread sundered to ground
   and
In a field grey lambs spring black hooves from
   wet grass green.

I MEET A SOLITARY ARCHANGEL

I slept and
  as I slept I dreamt and
What I dreamt was
  vision of a man
  projected into brightness of early
    crimson,
His body rising inclined into east,
Over the barren desert's mighty rocks
Three dark hours past dead Gethsemane.

Across empty declives and rushing winds strong,
Beautiful long and lean body with
  hands beside
  he rose into ethereal sky
Naked spirit, a piercing sword.

  I asked him my passing soul deliver,
  With awe and wonder
  Desired his will enfold me,
  A love strong as death.
  Adore.

Head turned on left shoulder
  Eyes carefully closed
  And
  He did smile a little.

SINS OF OUR FOREFATHERS ARE OF COMFORT

I.

The gladsome mind grows to golden air
    Shining frame.
Ancient of days, ancient of days!

Life's delightful play in living stream,
And the unbound spirits of our sons
    turn to song,

Sorrows cease.
    Joys ring,
Songs to sing the primal urges of our
    Forefathers.
Great grey-bearded heads of glorious patriarchs,
    Harvest grains.
Fathers, forefathers, fathers and fathers of our forefathers
    Great stones.
    Brightest day
Sons of the morning shaking heaven's high vaults until
    they ache.
Vernal breed in flecked air
    Pouring forth unstopped into the west.

Shoulders mighty, square,
    Massive
Swinging arms
    Body juices gay, not otherwise.

Flesh and blood.

Sweet odour,
    Sweat of large labours fleshed
        into veins of sweet liquor,

Wine, Whiskey, Women
Their bodies full, dark hair
Love and,
    The earth's roots and juiced vines.

II.

God grace this clay lest its blood run past
    its summer.
Sin and the jack devil genii in the desert,
Anvil-topped malign thunderheads growling
    through the lost land
And our weary souls their walls decay
        Foul water into stone,
    Thorns in our beds,
        Paled with anguished sorrow,
        Our loss.

III.

Ringing great throated horns belled,
    bayed beyond the frost
Our fathers' great heads in the dust.

    Wracked time
    Spoke forth in
Fierce strife, defied all foes. Death
    may die but not
    Forefathers whose sins were
    Harbingers of the human race.
Sin! Their cheerful songs across an
    Earth abased.

Their sins are of such comfort.
Outfling the first thrown stone,
Outrage the shame of pointed finger.

44

Scathing sceptres imperial in life's
Colourful streams, scattered fierce cups before them
and laughed to heaven's delight,
   with delight.

Such comfort.

SEPTEMBER, 1954

I.

Time passed through the afternoon
   A gentle tender wind,
Across sun-spots three shades of afternoon
   Blurred edges dancing.
Death's wish in mid-afternoon's silence
   cruel,
The sun child's death,
Climbed down into Earth's hollow,
   The evening and forlorn, lonesome pavements.

II.

Not the intense light of midday
   blinding,
Nor the fresh early day, but
Lambent light of moon mixed with
   rays of setting sun and autumn's
     first
      Cool.

Old moon with pared edge,
A light fades barren
Through the tired eye of man.

45

LATE SUMMER'S EVENING STAR

There is no lovelier Star.
There is no lovelier star than the early evening
   star of late summer
      Nor place to go in immortality.
Rich, vibrating, globose, clear
   Yellow and so near as to
     be
Closer than most agonies,
Farther than most sorrows,
Sweet star.

DEATH IN THE PRAIRIE OR DOORWAY, CHICAGO

Mortal man dead, a bundle
Through the doorway seen,
The distance diminuendo
   to horizon's infinite diverging lines
   driven into point.

Death on a prairie.
Shines noon with men in black coats,
Starched shirts,
Sitting stiff by coffin's edge and
Women with more calico colour than faces drained
in teared sorrow,
   Standing.
Unwrought through time.
Death in a doorway bundle
City streets webbed in prairie
The empty house doorways,
Death in a prairie city
Cheap talk and gaudy roast beef.
Family sanctuary.

LOVE ON THE R.R. IN BEDROOM WITHOUT SOFA

Lights on Jersey shores
Train from New York to Baltimore and
   time sad in between.
Dead sunflowers on stalks leaf stripped,
   Wastes of storms slashed across their heads.
Brick walk ends, bricks broken wet spaced.
Dried goldenrod plumes dusty brown
   blown, bent in the scant autumn winds
Bois-des-arc seed balls fan placed beneath thorn tree.
   Green apples still on their
   tree leaf stripped.

Station bare and few people, Thanksgiving's past,
   the Puritans have departed leaving
   us our musk-ox.
The dirty station parted by trains beneath the waves
   and emergent on Jersey shores midst lights
     swirling
Hollow damp tube and cave behind.
   The glory of lights
Ordered on banks, marching from water's edge
   Where steam is lit beneath light 'neath
   White stered steam, coils and recoils leaving
Our love unguarded and in possession of,
Red and chrome made clean by
   new darkness.
Parting the shores behind and lost in the dark dusk
The bedroom without sofa.
   And the sputtering arcs hanging outside beyond.
'What is this?
   Read it to me since I cannot clearly see.'
'Koronex, and Trigger, Shot 6,
   Chemicals, Gas and Steel.'

The untouched love
The new known.
Last cream rose of late summer
    caught in autumn's dew
        and held amid,
Gold red love of leaves
    Which lay upon green of rose bush,
Across late lawn's dew moisture.
Held in restraint, bitter, by first cool
    turning.
        Wild cherry leaves.
Single fruit burst and spilled its
    sticky seeds blood.
This beauty of movement, swift, then paused
    of flower, fruit, and moist place.

I have still summer's perfect mould
Though the mist and cold break it
                                away.

I love you so, contessa.

VIOLENT TRAIN

Violent train thrust seventy-five steel tons, of steel head
    forward,
Child's rhythm of choo-choo forgot and
    replaced by smooth flowing steel and diesel.
Start, brief pause, then across all Iowa,
    Illinois and Ohio.
Life rings from out its poles and enters the lists!

Now turgid slow the train moves.
    Large trees lie in parallel lines,
    Boles smoke blue,
    in their giant
        fall.

With sudden vigorous spurts
   against
   the intact forces. Now,
Quiet in mid-morning, not with a
  horn's blow
But sliding in and out of small towns,
     Slips.
   Carrying people in and out of country,
   In and out of town with or without pause.
The tree lines falter here,
Grey wood building scattered and
Shattered debris and man filth
  Cans, papers, ashes, machine entrails sharp broken,
Corn husks scattered, blown on ditch bank
  Winter's trees without leaves,
  Not wintered.
Streets fan from train into short mid-distance
  And run block against
Red and blue striped barrels, piles of
  Poles tar-dipped and ends lithopone,
Blue jeans hang upside down on line,
  three pairs hanging and praying.
Figures pass serene
Their faces untouched by steel-weighted thrust.

VERSE THIRTY-FOUR

I thought through all immediate bitterness, pain,
  Tried to source and discover
    And hence escape.
Knew not, found not the weal to lighten.
    But
To look across the plains of ages
  And see the folded cloths of
          death.

The body clean-scented and stark
  on bier
  with sweet unsoiled satin draped
    and
The friends who do walk by
  Without sorrow, remorse or music gay,
  But know the dead.

To be then burned clean, bone fragments and
  thus quickly return, through flame,
  the body's ordered, prized organic possessions.
  Its make content and compounds largely
    unto nature's
  cycles of nitrogen, hydrogen, water
    and copper blue.

Leave behind no spear of poison,
Enter emotionless estate.

Carry no pent-up sons
No tears of seminal death,
But the sapphired stone of sleep
  With fired heart.

Lost woman's love. Lost man's.
  No land,
    No Time,
      Nor Being
      Forever again.

PART II

FRAGMENTS

ff.   This most cruel of all eras,
    Man to man screwed into his most negative and destruc-
        tive worst.

ff.   Sandgap and Horsehead creek,
    The Town. The Morning's cock-crow spreads over.

ff.   Bare marked roots of trees
    Where kids kick and play.
    School-yard stumps.

ff.   Side by side Dark Plowed and Unplowed earth,
    The Plowshares shine.

ff.   Cocks fighting in the brittle dawn.

ff.   Fixed warrior on walking horse
        Frozen in time,
        in bronze.

ff.   There is always the road to Ephesus, twenty miles. To
    Ephesus Chapel, twenty and one half.

ff.   Symbol of war. The old army greatcoat, thick and brown
        with wide
    belt, shabbily worn on all roads, along roads.

ff.   The woman's body a crocus in the spring
        a flame tip.

THE RETURN

The woman dies due to the malign influence of a cold star.
The destinies
    Splendour.
The cathedral of the great beds
Massive
the place whence the race is made.

The bough is pistil of the tree
    carries its self in dark winter
In spring its small knots give green shoots,
Soon leaves, then buds and
Flowers follow to be by late summer.
Gold-tinted bough.

When down paved streets the people came
The automobiles are gone, grass grows
in the widening cracks, and people
    barefooted,
horses and cows, flocks of
    animals and fowls.
    young women walking forward
    young men vigorous whirl in the
    dance and cry the cry of the wild
    thing, feel the goat thrust
        and cry with bronzed throats and tongues.
    Music cries and sobs, Spring
The men with machetes, stones, guns, bombs
    are gone.
The voices of men return alive and singing
    to the new dawn, new moon silver in
    the morning west.
        It is there,
            not all destroyed but instead
                the green of life,

        Come, sing. Make a shrine there is
            a new God.
        To be loved!

ff.   First appearance of the Mask.
                For every soul accused, condemned,
                He picked up a dozen olives.
                He ate a black one for The East,
                He ate a green one for The West.

ff.   You have long narrow bones.

ELKHORN

At this brilliant lustrum
The grey clad and ragged died,
Without honour, without glory.

Split-minded, paranoid
Self-destruction to send
Human flesh to be
    clawed, chewed
    by the machine
    canister and grape.

Baptism of what?

At the end of cold marches.
To stand forward
Feel the fire of death spray
    the head.

Run a few steps
    Falter, run, die.
Battlefield.
The wood, the hills,
The springs.
The hidden cannon
    flash of bayonets
    flesh to rot.

OCTOBER 10, 1956

ff.   Live by our swords
Forget not the flame
   and
Turn swords, when forced
Into plow steel
   And forget not the flame
   And forget not the sword
   And forget not the earth!

ALDEBARAN AND THE ROMA WHITE WINE BOTTLE BEHIND THE DOOR BUSHES

Red giant and eighty light years with
   soft glowing companion
The old man puts his white pint wine bottle half
   empty
Behind the bushes beside the door.
   The old lady garrulous—

Brightest star in the V harrow of heaven,
   Weighing the lower limb with
      brightness.
With delicious sundered light.

COLOPHON

High colophon courts of the sun
Women in coan garments
With man's head bared.

The cop crosses the dark cavern'd store-house
The sun light strikes his head
Badgeglint on chest.

Stride.

Lens soften the mid distance,
Brown in the near.

56

CRY NOT FOR THOSE WHO BURN IN THE FIRES
OF TENDER HELL

Near Nirvana.
Pillars that are people stand in
   columns stolid,
Waiting entry into Hell.
   Or flail in tortured anticipation
     of the joy to flaunt
   Their vapid role as
Scillitan martyrs, before the waiting others.

My bones shan't cry for
   thee,
Nor hurt again when all flesh is gone
   therefrom.
The heather blows stiff
   and
Maundering into fires beyond.

CLOCK AND CLOGE

Time a membrane stretched by
   this man.
Moving in cluttered clock and cloge
   in our Time.
Time and real Time and make believe Time
   Shattered into
     and scattered by
   Strife.

The real, the unreal,
   good Time and/or the Bad.
The sharpened mind fogged, its edge gone
   by Time.
   The years are enough.
Corrosive enough, the hardened artery ways narrowed,

The fuzzed reflex.
No make-believe, Time.
Time is make-believe straight from the mind.
Draw a blank,
Use a camera. Catch Time.
Time of today. 12 ought noon.
The fear of Time lost.
Manacle Time, values of all
Time between present and past
A thin tight membrane, to break to be broken.
You are free
You return to the beginning.
Clutter of Time.
All move through Time's freedom
Time's loss.
Communicate, flow.

CRIE THE PHENIX

I am the fire
The fire is inside me
    it burns.
I call to those who here stand
    and all others
Come to the crimson phenix
Challenge the red fire
        I crie!
From the altar ashes my flame
    eternal crimson-red.
From the aromatic old roots
Springs the globe,
        of life.
Sun-worshipper this
    flame timeless
Indestructible stands above,
    beyond you indestructible,

everlasting, deathless, immortal,
   Young soul.
Saved from death and flood
   for all time.
Nature's reversal renewed in
   phenix
Life of all living stilled,
   burst forth in flame, the phenix.
Death close to life bought with
   other coins,
Death from the Scorpion sting of
   man's device
Restored by the phenix cry!
   mode of time to make the wonderful net
   rete mirable!
Day of Yalweh and of Thoth
   End entropy! Life born by
   Crie of the phenix.

FRAGMENTS

ff.   The girl child laughed
           wondrously!

ff.   Centaurs should be males
      or are males, so I thought
      until the day in Mannheim
      where I met a female. A problem,
    Unless, ah, yes, was—
    That's how it should be.

ff.   The shocked orchis and the red pain

ff.   Each of these lights on the Jersey Shore
      on the turnpikes will go under,
         mean more to me than
         any glory
         all glory
         than man could heap.

ff.   —and if this free spirit speaks
      let it speak!

59

—they had not sought the
golden hind
in the fields

other he would not be
adying,
Death lay in the
sunlight.

ff.   Years before the wars.
When ancient civilisations cast their own light before them.

ff.   Ripe fruit in atmosphere crossed with pollen
and dancing motes.

ff.   A raven walked carefully.

ff.   Orange coloured blossoms fall and stain the earth
rust red.

THE MASSED WORMPOT

They had rutted and slutted and gutted to their full,
The pavement is spotted with flow, their orifices.
Is it blood, vomit, urine, feces?

Look close at the moist spot which issues from mouth of
figure prone, his last living moisture.
The sidewalk is hard
The gutter is hard and dirty,
The vultures stalk until he is down.

THE STONE QUARRIES

Released
I will say these things
For one who lived in eras two,

Spanned half century.
Released
  to travel here and know
  To what foul usage
  they put our once-fine bodies
  in the stone quarries.
  In mode to ask the thing
    of
  placing man's body in slavery of toil,
    dirt,
      boxed by brutal labour
    into,
  senseless grift,
  with loins drawn
  straining against
  blind nature and
  cruel laws of man.

TRAIN AT CONESTOGA

Conestoga wagons to the west.
The stopped train with steam-burst boiler and
  the men standing with firelit faces
  repairing track and then engine.
A freight wreck in the wilderness not ten hours
  from New York.
The unexplained in life,
  the fragile
  the glass of life
  the repellent sight of
    sweated, panting woman
    reaching for a drink
    and a man on
    the fine stopped train.
Prepare your mind for this?
  We are past the wreck.

61

FIGURE IN A LANDSCAPE

A figure in a landscape,
Man in a landscape,
  stands upright, black figure
    in destiny clear grey
  stands and defies
      destiny.
When in this figure he goes West, stands
  narrow leg spraddle
  tight pants
  hand on belt to face
  death.
The figure does not move, stands
  unshadowed
  against the fallen late day-light
    or
Straight without shadow in
    midnoon
While the round of trains go fast
  past the hidden men
  hide indoors with fear and
  sudden death.

Wipes his face stares
  unafraid
  of the landscape with its
  FEAR and death traps.

The leather-covered westerner, tight-clothed body,
The loined body of the
  western warrior.
The scape is crowded with strangers,
  all stand alone.
  Alone in the universe
  endless landscape
    so great in array no
    man conquers

but upright man at once
universal yet separate, upright
in the vastscape
stands.
The colours, lights, beings change,
go away, leave alone the most significant
The deathless figure in landscape.

THE THREE-HEADED HOUND OF HELL

The wind notes change in the trees when
wind runs against new leaves,
Tree limbs move heavy.

What have we lost off this earth!
Solid physical objects and living things,
Great soldiers phalanxes of Samothrace,
The world's great wonders.
Ships, canals and more pyramids than remain.
People.
Languages unclaimed, lost.
The few remaining lines of Sappho!

PHIALE OMPHALOS

The knowledge of sorrow is a sting,
sorrow is another.
What man has placed in this
yet another.
Phiale omphalos and the tears shed,
flow therein
fill the cup.

Phiale Omphalos

Today without evidence
  the clay is
  evidence enough that
  all past man has had his sorrows
  of tragedy
    small
    or
    great.
Did hope by magic of the
  cup to know no more tears,
  To shed sorrow as tears, as ceremony.
  To know tears only as memory.

END